the blood runs from me
a poetry collection by Anne Pyle

this book discusses heavy topics such as:
- verbal harassment
- neglect and controlling parents
- psychological and emotional abuse
- abusive family members
- ableism
- generational and religious trauma
- pedophilia

please make sure you are in a safe, stable headspace before continuing.

to my new family:
you will never know how much you mean to me.

to my old family:
you will never know how much you did to me.

table of contents

part one
the blood

like a child

re: 1 Corinthians 13:1

when I was a child
I did not talk like one.
the words out of my mouth
pressured my parents
to kiss like playing house.

when I was a child
I did not understand like one.
simple things. stay away from dad,
he is angry, he will scream at you.
concepts grasped like babe's rattler.

when I was a child
I did not think like one.
wishing my brothers and I safety,
begging to stay out of trouble.
words considered like life or death.

now I am an adult.
I cannot put these childish things to rest.
instead I press them into these pages,
staining the book like coagulation.

I will not put the child behind me.
I will put her on display,
wring her of every drop of proof
and drench this book like gasoline.

to say his name

when I tell people about blood father
that he has touched countless others
but never laid a hand on me

when I tell friends about his screams
that they pierce my soul more
than my metalcore spouse's

when I tell counselors I fear his voice
that a single decibel raised
cascades me with trembles

I hear whispers deep within
that secrets should stay secrets
that blood is all I am

and all the shells on the shore
cannot silence their rush
within my beet-red ears

still with shaking hands I speak
the truth into the world

and each breath gets a little easier.

at three years old I was saved.
I was a bad toddler, and I was called to repent.

it was in my mother's minivan. I, in the very back,
called over to her, the driver, that I wished to be free
of sin.

and she believed me.

my earliest memory: I was terrified of hell.
little did I know how much more there was to fear.

apologetics

my brother wrote me a letter,
asking me what went wrong.
for things he did as a child,
for things he didn't remember.

he told me he was sorry

for things dad wouldn't recall.
like screaming at us children,
making me cry for hours,
like me, forgotten, again.

he told me he was sorry

when brother did nothing.
by not choosing a side,
he had picked the one
that hurt me the most.

he told me he was sorry

as if dad could be forgiven
for the crimes he committed.
as if a simple apology
would ever suffice.

they told me they were sorry

but it was an empty promise,
words falling short of meaning.
for how could they both possibly be,
if they know not what they've done?

I call them mom and dad.
titles, terms of endearment
to some. not to me.

hollow like a rotted oak,
mom and dad insist they
love me. their beloved child.

it's insulting how vast
they think their affection is.
how deep they think shallow is.

as if they both know who I am.
similar to how they shoved me
in a cage, called me pretty bird.

there is nothing left in me
that they celebrated. I'm not their
child doll to bend at will.

and I'm no fledgling either.
I taught myself to fly, and I
am never coming back.

good christian

they say hell hath no fury like a woman's scorn,
but what of a blood mother losing her control?

I still hear the echoes in my mind of her screech.
though the words are vague, one sticks out:

"goddamn" she yelled. her voice thin, crackling
as if the words themselves scorched her throat.

my mother never swore. I recall nothing worse
ever said than a good christian *crap. darn.*

to curse her god at me in one breath,
the facade dripping off her face like sweat.

I caught in her eye a glint of remorse
as if the word, in a moment of stress,

slipped, foreign, from her lips—
a serpent's forked tongue could spill no greater secret.

oddly enough, the context involved her wedding gift:
something I refused to take. a generous portion.

a good christian "take the goddamn money,"
the scream heard from here to Africa.

stephen hawking

my first memory of my dad
he ran to the bathroom coated in blood
an accident on the trampoline

my last memory of my dad
he skipped to my side coated in falsity
a forced *good to see you* and smile

the most pleasant memory
discussing time and space
one of few common topics left

the recollections in between
divorce and estrangement
uncomfortable and trite

every talk forced through
I always extrude conversation
until the very end

oh how they begged me
pleaded for me to call him
cried on hand and knee

but it is pleasant to recall
the space between us
as time expands

it is no falsehood
that never hearing from him
would be good for me

and it is no accident this time
that I have cut off my blood
never to parse memories again

just have faith

she lay there, a blanket chrysalis,
as I approached. eventually she stirred,
responding to my voice, as I rubbed
her back. after our brisk talk, I walked
away, letting her rest a day longer prior
to emerging as my schoolteacher, our
mother, and dad's codependent wife.

migraines marred her twenties and
thirties, the result of bearing the full
brunt of a family's worries and woes.
for a long time I pitied her for it, gave
her attention, care, a listening ear,
until I realized all of it was a choice.

the marriage she chose to continue. the
lessons she chose to self-teach me. the
brother she chose to overdiscipline. the
lies she chose to uphold and the cultic
classes she chose to attend that told her
she would never be good enough for us.

I have no more pity. I have only wrath,
that she chose piety over her own child
in a continuous act of self-flaggelation.

generations

I'm riding with my grandmother,
mother to my father, who raised
and poisoned him, as we passed a
member of their church. snow on
the ground.

I feel so bad for him, she says.
he married a person with autism.
what, I ask, makes that so bad?
she says they're like dogs. they
have no filter or personality,
or soul. they are machines.

she, who birthed a pedophile,
she, who raised an abuser,
feels shame for the spouse
of the autistic person,
as I feel shame for myself,
for being blood with a scorch
on the ground.

//

a few years later
I reunite with my grandmother,
to find her dementia teetering
forward, the cruel rose blossoming
in her mind, the thorns leaching into her.

she recites scripture, frowns at me
for listening to anything but hymns.
a simple ask, to see a bookstore,
skipping church to sightsee, on vacation?
a grave sin. she screams my scarlet letter.

to which her husband replies,
there are no christian bookstores left
in chicago. she does not hear.
he raises his voice. she does not listen.
he grabs her arm and shakes
it into her. only then can she mind.

//

I call my grandmother a few years later,
on christmas. I speak to her husband and
listen to him describe their son standing
there. they want me to speak to him. I

will not. they beg me to speak. I say
I have to go. they say he is reaching for
the phone, wishing me a merry christmas.
I hang up.

firstborn

like a bull in church, you
kicked off mother, reins lost.
responsibility and disrespect
warring in your broken thoughts.

you neglect a leaking mind,
your vigil seeping with lies.
the demons you whisper of
creep out your throat at night.

eye for eye, you castigate,
sticks and stones break me.
you bludgeon me with words
so husband wakes to my sobs.

tooth for tooth, you masticate,
chewing your cud of wrath.
your pain inside simmers,
boils over my unworn ring.

you taught me all I know,
the one I ripped out first.
you warned me not to regret
in love and self-defense.

I've grown to worry for you,
though I'll never turn back.
now to unlearn your ways
and close your bloodshot eyes.

something borrowed. something broken
in their mind.

a wedding. my wedding, and dad was
not allowed to touch me.

blood father poured wrath down the
pike. confidant informed.

we found out through blood brother.
a phone call. a scream.

my pastor walked me down. he understood
the risks. explained the illness.

the curse spread from one to another.
a bloodborne condition.

and yet, no one believed that union meant
relation. no one listened.

despite money flowing through broken pipes.
blind eyes to befriended ex-relatives.

to have, to hold, in sickness, in death.
they never seemed to understand.

a family that lacks the very things
that make up a family.

and a marriage they scoffed at
lasting longer than they'd ever feared.

blue screen of death

when I was twelve blood father promised to give me
his aged laptop, booted up black and green.
while he was away teaching I played the replacement,
a game built into the technology. when he came home
he screamed.
I winced at his tone, tears and snot pouring.
I'd hurt him. he'd broke me, snapped my will in twain.

the family grew concerned around dinner-time.
I, in my room, still bubbling. they prodded,
speak to her. we want to eat, bring her to dinner.
down the stairs I came, sniffing. could not look
him eye to burning eye. he said he was sorry. I'd get
the old laptop again, if only I'd come to dinner.

my stomach brimming with swallows of water and
mucus,
I was not hungry. had no desire to go. I did not
deserve to go.
punishment for my sins. atonement. I would stay, I
said,
over and over. I was not owed an apology, flinched at
touch.

love, redemption, food, all empty concepts. sins upon
sinner.

somehow the conversation resolved. somehow we
hugged.
somehow I left with them, still crying. somehow this
core
memory formed around us, of his scream, of my fear,
of me
standing at the base of the stairs, afraid to meet his
gaze as he
talked softly at me.

the old, beleaguered laptop never had a function.
I went over the screen, marveled at the fact that it was
mine, all mine, this new, functionless, featureless toy.
I hadn't deserved it, but I was given it: a lie, a yoke
to keep me trapped for a decade longer.

condemned

this family dances around the truth,
skirts it like two cars on a skinny road.

were it all to be revealed,
the light turned on and the skittering vermin
caught and inspected, would they turn on me?
do they resent being called what they are?

the secrets we hold within our lineage.
the truth we passed off as lies.
it builds up like scum in a sink basin,
to be scooped out and thrown away,
and yet they cling to it. why?

why do they let the water strain
through decades of filth?
why do they let the roaches crawl
on the floor and call their house
cleaner than mine?

nothing that I have done
compares to all the lies they hide.
strip away the paneling, find the
entire house is rotten. the foundation
is falling into the sand.

the doors are all locked on the inside,
and down they sink, into the abyss.
like crabs in a bucket, they refuse to leave
without the others. there will be no freedom.

not even the most innocent lamb
would make god pass over this house.

broken freedom

think too much
and it'll break me:

the computer
found in a corner

the past
lies we were told

the truth
lumped in our throats

the compartments
like post office boxes

the children
intracontinental

the life
we could have had

the age
barely older than me

the city
we will never go to

the thoughts
weighty on my mind

think too much
and it'll free me

I find it funny

how they put blinders around my eyes
and clog my ears with layers of wax
yet when I lose my grip on reality
they blame Satan and not themselves.

how they recite prayers and call pastors
when I say I hear screaming in my head.
how they curse the medication
when I say I'm doing better.

how they force me into hugs
when I tell them I'm hurting.
how they charge me rent
when I tell them I'm breaking.

how they reject my spouse
claiming found is not family,
but love how their blood
keeps in touch with ex-blood.

how they stop laughing
when they find out
I won't be their joke
anymore.

neanderthal

I cannot make a decision on my own.
I am simple-minded. I am neanderthal.
talk over my head. whisper behind my back.
it makes no difference to my brutish understanding.

my mind races in place. accursed treadmill.
I listen to the river of thoughts in my mind.
no one believes the truth, so why not trust a lie?
mental illness sprouts until it grows out my ears.

stupid girl, stupid foolish girl who went to college
to get a useless degree. followed her stupid heart
which led to him, the foolish boy.

did I really think I would listen to a boy
who told me I was more than what they said I was?
more than a forgetful girl with a pointless degree,
built to serve and be controlled?

my mental health was more than a curse,
greater than a demonic presence. no, this was
a hospitalization waiting to happen, pending
over and over again.

I never expected to grow older. how could I,
when all the things I sought in life were cast
away like chaff in the wind? when my interests
were uninteresting to the familial majority?

why should I have told them what I truly wanted
when they told me everything I should be?
when would I live up to their expectations?

so instead, I called myself names, as the littler
I made myself feel, the more attention I received,

until I was a pinprick of a person and they were
untenable giants in my eyes.

when I finally acted out of turn, when I cut
myself out of the tiny mold they'd cast for me,
they reacted in fury, saying I was the odd one out,
that I needed to crawl back in and stay there.

the blood is never content to let me be. there is
always more I must do. more I must achieve.
like quicksand, they suck me in again, again.
and I, the neanderthal, fall for their tricks.

I went to college freshly seventeen.
I skipped a grade at a young age,
hyperlexic and craving knowledge.

(she was this age when we found out.)

at the beginning it was simple.
painfully so. I was bored, inattentive.
it was too easy to forget it all.

(a threat of death told to her blood.)

I filmed myself walking around campus
at 1am, crying my eyes out, and posted
it on my blog for my social circles to see.

(the threat: a lawsuit to our family.)

I have no friends, I claimed, ignoring
lovely people I'd laughed half
the night away talking to. charades.

(her mother called mine that fateful night.)

in the morning she called to tell me I was
coming home. I begged and pleaded to stay,
at least til the semester ended. video a farce.

(dubious age of consent.)

I felt better in the morning. subsisting on
cookies and sink water. thanksgiving
break I'd showered once in a week.

(he tricked the cops.)

she was so concerned by christmas
I was to stay home for the break.
I agreed, though not given a choice.

(no one knows the truth, not even me.)

a couple months in I was sent to hospital,
to return zombified for a few years. doctors
didn't know what to do with me.

(what happened to you, neighbor boy?)

finally balanced on medication, I lost track
of time. memories slipped through fingers
like dust. learned truths a veneer.

(I made it out alive. that's what matters, right?)

the lies

"You can tell me anything."
"I know I can trust you with this."

"Your dad's working late tonight."
"We have to move; he's too stressed."

"We can't afford to eat out."
"Money's really tight right now."

"I just want you to be healthy."
"After everything I've done for you?"

"We want what's best for you."
"We love you just the way you are."

"I don't remember, but I'm sorry."
"They aren't family to me."

Lies sound so tempting to believe
when they're all you've known.

But one day, you'll wake up
and see the truth of who they are.

And when that day comes,
no one will hold you back.

security questions

I don't know what street I lived on or what my best friend's name was when I was a child. we moved so many times I can't count homes on both hands.

people ask me why that is. for a long time, I tell them it's from blood father's stress, until I learned the truth. now I'm afraid to answer.

things I remember from being young are so sparse. the pain sticks out like a sore thumb, but the happy moments fade into oblivion.

I don't know who blood father is behind all his lies, or what really happened to all those children. I don't know how to be happy, or how to release my anger.

I crawl into a new cage, huddle in the corner, and wait—for what, I can't tell. maybe someone will rescue me. maybe I'll rescue myself.

the blood runs from me

this is supposed to be my number.
the bit where I share my deepest,
darkest secret and regret. where I
delve into the most painful part,
rip open the covers with a scalpel
and bare the sickly soul of me.

my mind is a maze of memory.
anything prior to adulthood
shifts like sand, or the hot haze
on a faraway road in summer.

they will tell me stories of my
happy, sad, heartwarming,
rending memories and I sit
and nod as if a stranger.

I don't know all there is to me.
I look through a stained-glass
window as my kin inside
flit to and fro, wordless, with
only testimony to guide them,
only rumors to guide me.

I'm never been like most people.
most people, I'm told, are a tapestry
of recollections. the childhood stitched
together with movie quotes and dreams.

if that is the case, there is someone,
deep-dark inside me, who remembers.
I rake my arms, veins thirsty for her return,
but the blood runs from me.

part two
the found

found mother

I remember the first time I met her.
we were in an unknown town
at a familiar Tex-Mex restaurant.
the waiter came with green sauce.

she was larger than me, and kinder.
I, like a stick, hesitated to take a bite
of the seasoned chips and buttered salsa.
sitting next to my boyfriend of two weeks,

something in me was blaring. some sort of
panic reaction, flight engrained in my heart
as it fluttered with new emotions, new feelings
that I never knew I could feel before

but still, I stayed. I ate a chip, I ate two
and watched as they had their meals:
the mother and son, so similar, so strange
to my strangeness, foreign to my foreign.

I sat and watched and fought the urge
to get out of there while I still could.
I sat and ate and watched and thought
that maybe this could last forever.

wild inside, I mistrust affection
for an age. emotions wash over me
as love stays at my side, holding my hand.
he never hurt me.

he is a boy then, at twenty.
he patiently prunes back my
thorns, my thistles and choking
weeds, somehow knowing there
is a bloom somewhere inside.
he never hurt me.

the first time we hold hands,
I tell him I love him. yes,
it was a fledgling love, barely
a spark. it did not dwindle.
he never hurt me.

years pass. the ferality
wears off; I've grown
to flourish under his care.
a peck on the cheek. a tamed bird.
he never hurt me.

I didn't know what "cute" meant
until we spent an evening on my
dorm room bed, gazing into each
other's eyes, not even touching
each other—just unraveling
the hundred-layer wrappers
around my candied heart.

found father

he was a grouch, his wife promised.
a disgruntled man at the cusp of his fifties.
at christmas she dedicated a tiny tree to him,
the mean one, mister father-in-law.

he got into arguments with his son.
politics, religion, civil rights, no topic
off-limit to broach time and time again,
much to the chagrin of the missus.

he refused to preach at our wedding.
instead he provided the food, hiding
in the periphery, left to be so he
could cry his eyes out in happiness.

he tried to raise me like his own child.
newlyweds, we stayed under his roof
for a few years like little fledglings,
growing in love and kindness.

grouchy, argumentative, tender, caring:
all words we've used to paint the portrait
of the man I've come to know as a better dad
than I could ever dream of.

conditioning

unconditioning myself
ripping out the lies stitched into my mind
meticulously finding the truth

stripping down to the barest portions of me
looking at myself in the mirror
and teaching myself not to hate it

stipulations to keep myself safe
a nest at the top of the tallest tree
and the crabs left to fester in their bucket

tonight I'll prepare a meal
of foods I know by heart
and listen for the praise I deserve

and hope that one day
I can be free of their bonds
to learn how to love me

anniversary

I keep a mental tally from day one:
once we reach X years of marriage
we can tell everyone else to shut up.

the first year was the hardest
financial stress I'd ever known,
or perhaps known too well
for my age.

but throughout each year a certain
fear of making a huge mistake grows,
and as stressors rise, my fight or flight
born of trauma rears its head.

yet as I stay, as I brace myself—
for all I have ever known is pain—
it never comes. I am loved the same
today, tomorrow and the next.

so many hateful doubters
who have sealed their lips
throughout the years
congratulate me.

those in shorter relationships
promise me we're still in "puppy
love" more than six years in.

now, when we are just
as sweet and caring as day one,
sending *i love you*s across a room
or under our breath before we sleep,

there are no more dissenters.
no more backstabbers or pot-stirrers.

just him, me, and all the time in the world
to fall for each other more each day.

this is the one where I thrive.
where I flourish.
where I look back and think,
how did I ever let it get that bad?

past me had little understanding.
she didn't wonder why things got
so miserable. she let it all continue,
not knowing how much more there was.

now I have a loving, caring,
open-hearted family. now I have
a sweetheart spouse. now I have
disowned all the ones who hurt me.

now I must forgive myself
for not knowing any better.
for looking forward and thinking,
could I really have it that good?

traveling

I look out the window
as we go on a road trip
listening to your music
as you scream along
and my heart
oh my heart
is so full it could burst

so many of our memories
are formed during travel
and so many times
I have ended up shocked
simply impressed
by how gentle you are

the time I pissed myself
twice in one night
while driving us home
and you softly said
you would help me
clean it all up

and how many times
have you cleaned me up
after my blood family
left my heart bruised
and broken

you are everlastingly
patient, somehow,
after all that I have
put us through
after all they have
done to me while I
made you sit idly by

you are my protector
my tried-and-true love
and I won't let them
trample us any longer

I was once in a cage. I didn't know how to fly away.
they clipped my wings, tied the door shut.
told me I was a free spirit.

and then you, oh you.
you didn't yell, you didn't fight. you merely opened
the door,
and offered a single finger, and waited.

my wings were clipped, and you guided my flight
feathers
into growth. my talons were chipped and you
splinted them.
how patient you were, and are.

when finally I could soar above the world,
leave behind everything and everyone I had ever
known,
you drove alongside me.

I burst out, like a force of nature.
took up space and refused to listen
to the words and ones that hurt me most.

the bloods may curse your name,
blame you for all the decisions I made,
but I know the truth:

you are the one I trust
to help me
find my way out.

I have everything I've ever wanted:
a caring, loving husband
kind, thoughtful best friends
and a sealed-over hole in my heart
where blood used to live.

the founds have found me,
scooped me up and placed me
on a perch, and they proclaim
this is our lovely daughter
to anyone who will listen.

and I take everything they will give
and give everything they will take
for they respect my limits
and never limit their respect
and I have never felt so free.

it was a long time before I trusted he wouldn't leave.
that when he was angry it wouldn't be at me.
that the love wouldn't die, dry up over the years.

it was long, and not without error. many a time crying,
fearing that his raised voice was the end. that I was
unforgivable. that the marriage would be annulled.

but time and time again, he broke through the distrust,
not with violence but with patience. a kind, gentle
waiting. something I didn't expect: care.

it wasn't the kind I grew up on. I didn't know it
like I knew agony. I didn't recognize it the way I
did betrayal. even still, he persevered.

and in the end, after years of nothing but the deepest
tenderheartedness, I stopped idealizing my past.
started feeling the churn of emotion in my dead earth.

he and I were now *us*. a united force against
all the cruelty of the world that blood had sown
within me, had taught me to crave.

my farmer, plucking the weeds of doubt, planting
and watering my love for him, just as a rose in
our own front yard.

and somehow, he won the war with my trauma,
and who I am now came to fruition. he cradles
my blooms and cuts off the dying brambles.

we reap the spoils of my grinchian heart,
grown three sizes larger under his tender care.
love turned gentle, growing like a weed.

on that fateful day,
when I cut off all my blood,
I felt nothing but peace.

grief followed, the greasy slimy
kind that coats all your memories
with sorrow and fondness.

I can't explain the bittersweet
taste in my mouth that refuses
to leave the more I spit it out.

as much as I condemn, I can
never be fully rid of them.
they live on in memory.

strange what insults I recall.
what pain I miss, despite
how much it crushed me.

but as time passes,
I enjoy moments alone with
only founds to embrace.

two years later and I am here,
feeling more whole than ever,
peeling back layers of trauma.

I have overcome so much
pain and sorrow and heartbreak.
and all that's left is me.

what I deserve

it was hard to imagine it being anything.
that I should have nice things just because I existed.

my blood told me it was nothing, that I'd have to work
by myself to get anything I wanted.

my founds told me I could have whatever I desired.
that they'd help me reach it.

but what was it that I wanted, with all my heart?
oh yes, others deserve the world, but me?

self-esteem was never my strong suit, crushed by
blood's hands a thousand times over.

yet my dreams still sprouted, even at a young age.
I'd wanted to be an author for ages.

my bloods demand recompense. that I receive
what I truly deserve.

I demand it too. and I receive it, time and time again:
the love of others who see me as me.

what did the preacher say

I describe my blood as a cult, as is their paradigm.
a deity who only let a select few into heaven,
depending on how hard we worked.

after a while in freedom, I learned this employer
did not exist the way I was taught.
there was no control factor.

there was only one factor that mattered,
the one my bloods refused to acknowledge:
grace, the potency of which rocked me.

instead of a god who demanded subservience,
who punished disobedience and declared
every human on earth unworthy from birth,

I decided to believe in a biblical figure.
a person who socialized with the outcast.
a man who would have chosen me.

ironic how the man the bloods killed
is the same one they claim to love,
when they sent him to hell, too.

on purity culture

I'm not a piece of tape. I don't lose my stickiness
after use. I'm not something to even be used.
I don't rot over time. I don't become misshapen.
that portion of me is not to be discussed from a
pulpit.
not to be projected from a blood who sat me down
with
shitty '80s tapes on celibacy to digest and internalize.

when I first got married, I thought the burden placed
on virginity would dissipate. instead, it intensified.
I, in a stable, monogamous relationship—the
supposed
pinnacle of safety in relations—could not let go of the
shame. somehow this purity culture stuck with me,
made me deserve to torture myself.

blood-kins told me similarly. that anything done
without my husband's involvement was wretched,
a sin. a sin to explore myself by myself. a sin to
take certain positions. a sin to believe that sex was
more than something to endure for his pleasure,
his alone, to be manipulated, used, taken away.

when I let go of the belief of what sex meant,
walked back the decade of manmade
commandments,
pushed against the role I was constructed in life and
love,
and settled into who I was supposed to be for him,
there was more trust than a million vows could
contain.

upon meeting new people, I have to answer
two questions most prevalently:

do you have kids? and
what are your blood like?

it comes naturally to new people.
populates easily on their tongues, the

words that hold the most weight
to me. the most common pain.

I don't have kids due to fatigue and
mental illness. I don't have blood

because they cursed me with both.
latter perpetuates the former.

I have been told over and over
what a good mother I'd be.

I have been told time and again
how blood is blood.

others with painful backgrounds
vent their frustrations at such questions

and allegations. we beg to be free
of the compulsion of parenthood.

we hold our bloods accountable
for how they have harmed us.

our pursuit of healthiness
the public finds repugnant, but

I'd rather be an orphan by choice
than a martyr at their hands.

trust in a lie

you would not believe
the things I've been told
in the name of love,
as if I'm clueless to its touch.

the more I listen to the way
the founds think of me,
that we celebrate differences
and care without consequence,

the more I am convinced
that my blood don't even love
me, merely the idea of me.
a concept, an empty shell.

who I am now, proudly,
is someone they wish I wasn't.
they've expressed often they
miss who I used to be.

is irony lost on them,
that I am more myself than
ever, that who they knew
was only conformity?

fight, flight, freeze, fawn—
I memorized all the tactics
handed down to me
for survival within the pack.

and that was all my mind knew.
even at my happiest moment,
I was holding back to conform.
praised for their negligence.

all the terms used to describe me.
an old soul. mature for my age.
why couldn't my brothers be more
like me, the traumatized teen?

I had to unlearn all the pain,
all the toxic traits they'd
branded into my side
until it became osmosed.

with dish soap and care,
I scrub through my feathers,
remove the trauma oil spill
saturated down to my skin.

if only the black tarry stains
would wash out as well
with the filthy bubbly water
I dump down the drain.

satisfaction

that time in the car
when I sobbed my eyes out—
knowing I'd have to give up
the one good part the pandemic
had given me—did you think
I'd lost my mind?

this cat, a simple feline,
fitting into my arms like
a forgotten friend, taught me
more than the age of heartbreak
had settled into my soul.

I'd had most things I loved
taken from me, through time.
if it weren't a pet, it was toys,
happiness, games, adventures,
all stripped away like prometheus'
innards, day after day after fucking day.

you consented to keep her,
listened to my pleas and pardoned
my pendulum of mood swings
as I let out my emotion from
feeling triggered by blood father.

the day that I exploded in the car
with blood father and brother as I
ate a burger, med-withdrawal coarsing
through my veins, I'd never felt so
unlike myself, so othered.

the same action that you forgave,
they nailed into my coffin.
the same fear I experienced

leaked into their visages and
eked away under your care.

how did you know what I needed
when I needed it most?
and why did they, embodied in
failure, proclaim that you
were my mortal enemy?

the truth is,
there is no end.

trauma and pain and grief
don't turn off.

healing knows no bounds.
layer upon layer of bruising,

down to the very bones of me,
through the marrow.

the bullet wound healed over.
I dig through to the center;

even when the bullet is removed,
shrapnel finds its way

into my organs. the scar tissue
forms around them.

after the surgeon. after the
therapy. relearning who I am.

beginning to function without
parts I thought were essential.

without people I thought
would always be there.

//

I remember the first time
a patient died during my shift.

I remember the screaming
and banging on the wall.

the parents. the siblings.
the sobbing went on for hours.

it was then I learned
what grief really was.

it was then I knew
what the cost could be.

but even with it,
after all my emotional

turmoil rocked my vessel
to its very core,

I know that ripping out my heart
was the right decision.

//

so no,
this is not the end.

this is a brand new start,
a rebirth of sorts

where I can find
new family to rely on.

family that doesn't hurt me
when it claims to love me.

family that apologizes
and accepts apology.

I control how the story flows
this time.

and I will make sure
it is full of hope.

acknowledgements

First and foremost, I must say a huge gift of thanks to my "founds," the Pyle family, for taking me under their wing as one of their own. Especially Jacob, my husband and inspiration, without whom none of this book would have been possible.
To my online home, the Salty Cult Writing Family, and to all its members, who keep me going when all I want to do is give up.
To my friends: Katie and Miranda, who cheered me on when all felt lost. Lisa and Lyn, who provided helpful feedback and encouragement. Amanda V., who cheers me on. Micah L., who gives me something to look forward to. Hazel, who has been with me through thick and thin. And to all who set up and attended my book announcement surprise party.
To my psychiatrist, who helped me find myself.
A special shout-out to Shelby Leigh, my editor; to Meesh, my cover artist; to B. Evans, my cover designer; and to Sarah Dorsey, my photographer: thank you for sticking with me once more.

9 7 9 8 9 9 9 6 0 7 9 1 1 7